Outside the Box

Teams

Kristy Stark, M.A.Ed.

Publishing Credits

Rachelle Cracchiolo, M.S.Ed., *Publisher*
Conni Medina, M.A.Ed., *Managing Editor*
Nika Fabienke, Ed.D., *Series Developer*
June Kikuchi, *Content Director*
John Leach, *Assistant Editor*
Kevin Pham, *Graphic Designer*

Image Credits: All images from iStock and/or Shutterstock.

Library of Congress Cataloging-in-Publication Data

Names: Stark, Kristy, author.
Title: Outside the box : teams / Kristy Stark.
Description: Huntington Beach, CA : Teacher Created Materials, [2018] | Audience: K to grade 3.
Identifiers: LCCN 2017029994 (print) | LCCN 2017054043 (ebook) | ISBN 9781425853204 (eBook) | ISBN 9781425849467 (pbk.)
Subjects: LCSH: Teamwork (Sports)--Juvenile literature. | Cooperativeness--Juvenile literature.
Classification: LCC GV706.8 (ebook) | LCC GV706.8 .S73 2018 (print) | DDC 796.01--dc23
LC record available at https://lccn.loc.gov/2017029994

Teacher Created Materials
5301 Oceanus Drive
Huntington Beach, CA 92649-1030
http://www.tcmpub.com

ISBN 978-1-4258-4946-7

Printed by: 51497
Printed in: China

This is a team.

Teams play.

Teams work.

Teams learn.

Teams care.

What teams do you see?